Seed Poems

Compiled by John Foster

WITHDRAWN

Contents

Growing Cress	Stanley Cook	2
Seedy Story	Judith Nicholls	3
Scarlet Runner	Ann Bonner	4
The Ancient Oak	Ann Bonner	6
Acorn	Jill Townsend	6
Family Trees	Adam Coleman	7
Apple Seed	Judith Nicholls	8
Bread	H. E. Wilkinson	10
Harvest	Jean Kenward	12
Harvest Festival	Irene Yates	14
Seeds	Hilda I. Rostron	15
The Magic Seeds	James Reeves	16

Acknowledgements

The Editor and Publisher wish to thank the following who have kindly given permission for the use of copyright material:

Ann Bonner for 'The Ancient Oak' and 'Scarlet Runner' © 1990 Ann Bonner; Adam Coleman for 'Family Trees' © 1990 Adam Coleman; Stanley Cook for 'Growing Cress' © 1990 Stanley Cook; Jean Kenward for 'Harvest' © 1990 Jean Kenward; Judith Nicholls for 'Seedy Story' and 'Apple Seed' both © 1990 Judith Nicholls; The James Reeves Estate for 'The Magic Seeds' from 'The Complete Poems for Children' (Heinemann) © James Reeves; Jill Townsend for 'Acorn' © 1990 Jill Townsend; Irene Yates for 'Harvest Festival' © 1990 Irene Yates.

Although every effort has been made to contact the owners of copyright material, a few have been impossible to trace, but if they contact the Publisher, correct acknowledgement will be made in future editions.

Growing Cress

The cress seeds we planted
Were small as pencil dots.
We scattered them on soil
In white plastic pots.

It only took two weeks
For my cress seeds to grow
Into a thick green forest
In walls as white as snow.

Stanley Cook

Seedy Story

Saucerful of mustard seed,
jam-jar full of beans;
all we'll have to eat next week
is greens, *greens*, GREENS!

Sprouting seeds inside the dish,
I know what this means!
Sprouts and shoots and leafy tops
and greens, *greens*, GREENS!

Judith Nicholls

Scarlet Runner

I planted a bean seed.
I watched it grow.
I'll never know
how, from being so small
it got so tall.
It climbed up the pole
we'd stuck in the ground.
Up it went
round and around
until it seemed
it would never stop.
When it reached
the very top
it flowered – Red.
My Dad said
that those would be beans.
He was right.
We had them for dinner.
Tonight.

Ann Bonner

4

The Ancient Oak

How many
years
will it be
before this
little acorn
becomes that
huge
oak tree?

Ann Bonner

Acorn

Sitting in its fat little egg-cup,
Humpty Dumpty among the leaves
in its knobbly green trousers,
holding its tummy like a secret,
the secret of a new oak tree.

Jill Townsend

6

Family Trees

My grandad planted an apple tree
when he was just as old as me.
The leaves grow thick on grandad's tree,
but he's as bald as bald can be.

My grandma planted a cherry tree
when she was just as old as me.
The trunk grew tall and straight and thick,
so grandad made her a walking stick.

I've planted an oak.
By the time it's grown
I'll have grandchildren
of my own.

Adam Coleman

7

Apple Seed

There's an apple in my garden
and only I know where . . .

Leave the apple there!

There's a seed
in the apple in my garden,
it's small and bright and brown

Lay the seed down!

There's rain
on my seed
from the apple in my garden,
there's rain and soil and sun . . .

Let the rain run!

There's a shoot
in the rain
on my seed
from the apple in my garden
and two leaves on the shoot . . .

Let the small seed root!

There's a tree
from the shoot
in the rain
on my seed
from the apple in my garden,
and there's something on its bough . . .

Eat the apple now!

Judith Nicholls

9

Bread

'Farmer, is the harvest ready
For we must have bread?'
'Go and look at all my fields,'
Is what the farmer said.

So we ran and saw the wheat
Standing straight and tall.
'There's your bread,' the farmer said,
'Have no fear at all.'

'Miller, is the flour ready
For we must have bread?'
'Go and look in all my sacks,'
Is what the miller said.

So we ran and saw the flour,
Soft and white as snow.
'There's your bread,' the miller said,
As we turned to go.

'Mother, is the oven ready
For we must have bread?'
'Go and open wide the door,'
Is what our mother said.

So we ran and saw the loaves
Crisp and brown to see.
'There's your bread,' our mother said,
'Ready for your tea.'

H. E. Wilkinson

Harvest

Come and see
    the harvest,
come and pick
    the corn!
Make a dolly
    out of it,
one that's quickly
    born.
Turn her arms
    and twist her,
tie her
    here and there.
Now she's like
    a person,
with bright golden
    hair.

Thank you
      for the harvest,
thank you
      for the crop.
We will make
      a loaf of bread
with crust upon
      the top.
Here we come
      a-dancing
with a basket
      full of bread.
Come and see
      our dolly
with a crown
      upon her head!

Jean Kenward

Harvest Festival

Cabbages, cauliflowers,
  crisp, crunchy swedes,
  peppers and parsnips
  and melons with seeds;
Onions and mushrooms,
  potatoes for chips,
  tomatoes, bananas
  and apples with pips;
Stick beans and broad beans
  and beans in a tin,
  blackcurrants so juicy
  they run down your chin;
Cornflakes for breakfast
  and mangoes for tea –
Come to our harvest
  and give thanks with me.

Irene Yates

Seeds

Seeds that twist and seeds that twirl
Seeds with wings which spin and whirl;

Seeds that float on thistledown
Seeds in coats of glossy brown;

Seeds that burst with popping sound
From their pods to reach the ground;

Seeds with hooks that clutch and cling
Seeds I plant for flowers next spring.

Hilda I. Rostron

The Magic Seeds

There was an old woman who sowed a corn seed,
And from it there sprouted a tall yellow weed.
She planted the seeds of the tall yellow flower,
And up sprang a blue one in less than an hour.
The seed of the blue one she sowed in a bed,
And up sprang a tall tree with blossoms of red.
And high in the tree-top there sang a white bird,
And his song was the sweetest that ever was heard.
The people they came from far and near,
The song of the little white bird to hear.

James Reeves

Sally Kilroy